www.BeirBuaPress.com

Fragments from

before

the Fall

An Anthology of Post-Anthropocene Poetry

by

JP Seabright

Published by Beir Bua Press

*This collection is dedicated to all those fighting – in whatever capacity –
against the ongoing climate crisis and its impact on life on this planet.*

ISBN: 978-1-914972-28-7

Beir Bua Press, Co. Tipperary, Ireland.
Typesetting / Layout, Cover design: Michelle Moloney King
Cover image by Michelle Moloney King

Ordering Information: For details, see www.BeirBuaPress.com

Published by Beir Bua Press

Printed in the UK

Our printer is certified as a B Corporation to measure our impact on the
environment and help drive us to be even more conscious of our footprint.

9 781914 972287

INTRODUCTION

The texts contained within this collection date from the last throes of the Anthropocene era, around the time known to current historians as The Fall. Some are believed to originate from just before this global occurrence and some immediately succeeding. It is difficult to provide accurate dates for a period commonly known as the New Dark Ages.

Only four of the texts here are considered complete: the first, entitled *Fragments from Before the Fall*, is believed to have been pieced together contemporaneously making it a particularly thrilling find; the short pieces *Hunting* and *Weather* are also considered complete, as is the artifact entitled *CLAP*. This text, which some scholars claim originated from a diary entry posted onto the International Network, has the appearance of poetry but, like most of the pieces in this collection, one cannot be certain of the author's intentions. For this reason, it is hard to determine the original meaning or syntax, but the text presented here is considered more authentic than in previous collections.

The subject matter of *CLAP*, like many of the other texts contained within this collection, reference the first of several worldwide viral pandemics during the early 21st Century (B.F.). Other texts refer to similar contemporaneous events such as the first stages of global environmental collapse, the series of seismic shifts which heralded the post-Anthropocene era, known colloquially as 'The Fall'. This anthology presents a fascinating insight into humanity's reaction and response to these catastrophic events and provides an illuminating lesson for current readers interested not only in the history but culture of those times.

Where words are missing or indecipherable due to water or fire damage, they have not been added to the text; it is presented 'as found'. Where research has provided sufficient evidence of the author's intention, these words have been presented within square brackets. Similarly, where titles are not certain but are suggested from ephemera or notes found near or associated with the text, these have been placed inside brackets. Where there is insufficient evidence or certainty, titles have not been added, so as not to influence the experience of the reader's interaction with these rare found texts.

JP Seabright, Lúndūn, Year of the Fall: +09

Since initial publication of this anthology, further artifacts have been recovered from this pre- and immediately postlapsarian era, which shed important light on the context of this material. These have been added to later editions of this collection; their archival details provided in A Note on the Annex.
Publisher's Note, Xiǎofèi, Year of the Fall: +11

[Fragments from Before the Fall]

It begins   thin
                hairline crack
                        barely
                                fracture
                                fissure
                change [in]   pressure
                                        strangest   weather

Breathing   laboured
                bleed   easily
                    from
                                occasionally
                                    [then] daily
Hair falls
            fingernails loosen
                        splinter
                                sky darkens
                            as if [it is] winter

                wrong
            everyone
                            world   turns
                                bent [on]   axis
                        heavy   worn
                        wrong places

Holes   torn
                atmosphere
                            something [is] rotting
                                        smell [it] down here

                            *

Once   green
pleasant
            means not dying

[not] dirty   diseased
                    colour of uniforms
     brighter   cleaner

                        was woodland
      good place
                scarred battlefield
      charred corpses
                            chosen [to] burn themselves
[not] wait for   sun   scorch   to death

                nighttime   we slept
instead   world awakes
            left of it
          [to] survive somehow
                        glaring eye of [the] sun
We   be[come] troglodytes
          human worms

                              *

     blister   peel
                all black now
                    some darker
                              survive   longest
          Survival [of]   fittest
                          fit is
                slow
                    careful
                              cunning
                                  [calm]
                                        earthworms
                              *

     first   to the ice
                centre [was] dead
     little   left

          when   gone
the floods
                  welcome
respite   heat
                  many died
     winds   waves
                  consumed [the] land
     still   sun burnt
           through the clouds

     barriers
           fortifications
                desperate
           scientific experiments
[we] made   rain
                cool   down
but
                  burnt our skin
           hair fall out

Some   left
                ships [to]   stars
     don't know [if]   survived
                before   lines [went] silent
                  if we   [not] spent
                     on escape
could we   saved [the] earth
                     already too late

                                        *

                     we are   damned
                          last   lonely few
                     hunting [for] rats
                     fighting   scraps
                     fucking [for] bread
                man killed   can of coke
           not yet   devour [our] flesh
                     but [it] will come

[Mutation]

across the species barrier
food chain
shaking of hands
business meetings
hugs
child
open-mouthed kisses
teacups
flying sweat   dance floor
fruit [at the] supermarket
pub   post office
my face   yours
from being
touching
breathing

Girt by Fire

to the horizon
fires   still burning
smoke in the air
hearts

Embers   sky like fireflies
homes   lives

they did [not] come
help
still waiting
hope   gone

our holy land
charcoal smudge

The sea
trees are burning
burning
all burning

we stared
through   falling ash
the dying light

they did [not] come

[Correspondence]

      notes for each
    kitchen tables
     fridge
      food parcels
    unopened letters
for weeks

quarantined
  rarely   speak

discovered
uncovered [from] moss and masks
I   my dreams

[Contagious]

when you leave

Before the Fall
last breath
One last
death
chance

Forgive me

the virus
plague
death on my lips
Black mould [on my] lungs
White ash
always remember
contagious laughter

Spilt Milk

I found my love
when we still used
before it became
before our house
and we

I found her crying
months of worry
weeks of waiting
of refilling buckets
we never knew

I found my wife
a pool of white
her hands shaking
I'm sorry I'm sorry
it's only milk I said

[This text was discovered on paper ripped in half. This represents the left-hand side of that paper]

[…]

my breath

    fought for

bursts

    rib cage

imprisoned

struggling

fill up [with] water

  never imagined

    confines of my bed

[Herd Immunity]

          containment camps
  keep us safe
protect   from wind   rain
           assets

     corrugated hangar
  small pens   metal
  low troughs
    food   other for faeces
Water and piss   in plastic bottles
         resemble each other
  taste   [the] same

 given a number
luckiest   the middle
     exposed to   elements
       greatest chance [of] warmth   survival
   built for cattle
breeding   into burgers
    died of   madness
   [we] do the same

[Infanticide]

Kill it
    afford to keep it
      enough food
   survive   winter
       deformities
  always

     born normal
       lungs
  dysfunctional
   have lived
    seen and done?

she may [not] be deformed
she may
   it's possible
 can repopulate
    be the last

    or I will
How   I kill her
this baby

    to find
someone who   give
her food

      crying
  freeze to death
  smothered breath

take [her] last moments of
warmth
    under the dead tree
  hide
   devour her flesh

Weather

Snow falls over the city

      flakes of dust

Skin of others' lives and mothers' love

Snow falls like a blessing

      like forgiveness

Shavings of bone and blood

We open our hands to receive anointment

We open our mouths too
            for some
                  small

      semblance
                     of
         sustenance

We are all hungry now

[Driftwood]

I was

      dreaming

             holding you

      silently

             holding on

      hoping

              [keep] me from

           wrapped

                like driftwood

      trying

          afloat

[Carburetor]

Metallic screeching

        eardrums   unnatural

               something tortured

       to the same campfire

offering   shelter

          move on searching

        safer underground

   were large tracks across the land

               hundreds thousands

more than you can imagine

         What happened

               extinct?

      fire water special oil

         none   left

    carcass creaks empty

[Skin]

       skin cracked

     as rivers once

  memory of flowing water

              pipes   [taps]

     from the sky

        it falls it burns

does [not] quench [our] thirst

CLAP

scrip scrape
through earth
dirt
search for scraps
'thing to eat
swap
for meat
"clap for carers"
sign -
i found it
mine -
i keep
'thing to hold
o'er head
from heat
and cold
what is clap
i ask
ancient
burial rite
he said
'fore to send
dead to sky
now we burn 'em
where they lie

[Silence]

    roars in my ear
           static white noise
  weight   chest
                breath
      damp finger

            of death

the unbearable
        a blindness
nerves cut
           without sound
no sonar trace
        aural footprints
     empty echoes
      untethered weak   hollow

    with inarticulation

stuttering utterance
      fucking   impotence
empty
     burst
   sickness spreads
      Silence

Reveal-Redact

there was silence in heaven
    the prayers of all saints
                    ascended up
cast it into the earth   thunderings, and lightnings,
and an earthquake
              hail and fire mingled with blood
                trees was burnt up   all green grass
was burnt up
            the sea became blood   died
     ships were destroyed   there fell a great star from heaven,
burning
              many men died of the fire
    the sun was smitten
darkened
     flying through the midst of heaven Woe, woe, woe, to the
inhabiters   I saw a star fall from
heaven unto the earth
             the sun and the air were darkened by
reason   out of the
smoke locusts upon the earth   men seek
death, and shall not find it   shall desire to die
            One woe is past; and, behold, there come
two woes more
            men killed, by the fire, and by the smoke
which issued out of their mouths

    the men which were not killed by these plagues yet repented not of
the works of their hands

[birds fly backwards]

birds fly backwards
      fall to earth
            rain dissolves mid[air]
                  rivers dry up
                        parch the ground
                              desiccate the air

       *

      no time   bury our dead
   left   in [their] beds
           gasping   breath
      them [too]   no air left

       *

In   ether
          burnt metal
[Smolde]ring plastic
Melting leath[er]
     smell of dead hide
       fur
          skin
       in my hair
      clothes
   mouth   eyes

       *

[Disintegration]

      unravelling

Layer

         brick

I

Roof caved

        broken

Bones exposed

          shaken

      [im]ploding

          disintegrating

        weight of time

      whim of   weather

    collapsing

Lungs filled

Limbs detached

   empty   silent

   abandoned building

[Commodity Stock]

Cars

Cows   comm[odity]

Coke : a com

       pacemakers skin

Teeth [kidney] hair spleen

Genome spliced   stock exchange

    bloated corpses   hand-dug cess[pits]

[...]

                    At this
                            in time
                    everything

                    my hands

              turn it over

              right/left

              life/death

                        no choice
                    already
                            time ago
                    since
                        playing   time

                        of misfortune
                    laughing
                        [me]
            endless days   nothing

                    but

                    when
                    now
                    not
                    if

                turn it over
        long sharp [.....] edged knife
                    this point
                    life
                    death
                    [rite]
                    left

[Denouement]

skin burns
          feed [strips] of me to [the] birds
   meat   burned   charred
               in the sun
still no

              Hollywood end[ing]
            reprieve
   dramatic rescue
          escape
   revenge
      in reverse
leave [you here]   die

          nothing
just you
      rotting   sun

you
     Don't leave
       free to go

   I don't
             after all [this] time
     release me

[After Words]

       hordes of locusts

burning rivers

birds drop

  seas rise   dies

Like the bible

   the plague another

      end times say others

     it was

This is after

    Time

[blood rust]

Blood rust [runs] deep
    break down
Speech for
     needed
   of life
Un
      too much content
       unreal
Fake new
         that last century
     RIP of human[ity]
   many words
Not
     voices
Not enough

Miasma

curve of   world
        curling around
                snaking   me
                        doubling
                                poison tipped arrow
                                        in[to] my mouth

                                I swallow
                        swallow   down
            poison   all
        radiating
chemical   venomous
        snakebite [and] black
                curling
                        doubling

                        breath [in] miasma
                                lungs protest
                                        cry [for] oxygen
                                                struggle
                                        breath
                                                putrescence
                                incandescent [with] death
                                        wreathed   decay
                                        cells collapse
                                        effluence
                                I lack
                                curling
                                        back
                truth of   world

                roof [of]   mouth
                        burning   bubbling
                                poison   arrow
                                        out of [my] breast
                                                curdling
                                        choking
                                throat constricts
                        tongue turns black
            curling
                and doubling

Hunting

we run

    under cover of wet skies

and hurricane winds

    it's easier to hunt the haunted at night

in the dark everyone shines

    the whites of our eyes

showing the way we've come

    and how far we have to go

[...]

                    words fail
            scraps [of] paper in   wind
                    under my foot
                    before

                            contaminated
                    turned   inward
            insular ig[norant] stupid

                    words melt
                        twisted plastic over metal
                    origins deleted
                                    something
                new   terrifying
                                other
                            obsolete
                            void

    writing these words not [for my] future self

            my previous existence

            who we   were
                    different time

        Our daughter lies between us
                    had not made her

        words   glutinous in our mouths
                    unspoken accusations

[The End Is Night]

We will find

futile attempt   prevent
descending further
depression

was the worst
the end
we were wrong
collapse
starting point

only in hindsight
too little

scrap of paper
THE END IS NIGHT says
T [in] black charcoal

the typeface
how true
The End is   Night
darkness every day
out the sun

[Before the Fall]

Before the [Fall]
    gods   our own
        made them known
            [no] longer afraid
Everything   explainable
              understandable
          chose not
   follow   science
           no excuse [for] ignorance
[I] remember these days
How quickly   when it comes
          we forget
    nothing   anymore
     warnings
   evidence was
Why did
Why

[After Party]

                the last generation
                        chosen few
        Generation O [for] Omega

                we [are] out of time
                        beyond time
                watch   skies
                            why they wore
                time [on] their wrists
                measured   moving hands
                        numbers
                which increase
                start again

                        Post Anthropo-Scene
                [the] After Party
        Terra Nullius once more

A NOTE ON THE ANNEX

Since the initial publication of this collection, an incredible find in the waterlogged basement archives of the Koninklijke Bibliotheek (the National Library of the Netherlands based in the underwater city of Den Haag) has shed light on the global circumstances of when the material in this anthology is believed to have been written. These have been discovered by the editor and are presented here to offer cultural and historical context to these pre-Fall poems. It is hoped that future historians will be able to reflect on the lessons that these rescued documents offer.

The first, designated the archival record [ipcc.ch/sr15] is believed to relate to an intergovernmental report (when such cross-border communications were still possible) regarding the planetary climate crisis. An extract of one of the most pertinent sections of these retrieved drowned papers is included here, and relates to historical evidence that the widespread and irreversible impacts of global temperature increases were widely known and communicated at the time. This makes the lack of action and attempts to avert the catastrophic impact of The Fall even more astonishing.

The second piece, added to this anthology for further context of the living conditions and concerns of the proletariat during this time, is a printout from the International Network, circa 2021 C.E., entitled *[searching for answers]*. Historical evidence suggests that this was produced at the same time as the release of the global warming report. Despite the clear scientific evidence demonstrated in this report, even from the excerpts and fragments available to us now decades later, this suggests an extraordinary lack of awareness and commitment from the general population.

The two extracts are presented as found. Whereas it is unfortunate that much of the text in Annex 1 is illegible due to water damage, the editor and publisher of this anthology consider it to be a significant historical find that complements the other work in this collection.

A1 : [ipcc.ch/sr15]

new scientific
evidence   natural and human
systems   magnitude   pattern of risks
1.5°C above   pre-industrial period
            Warmer Worlds
organisms   ecosystems   human
well-being
            frequency and magnitude   Human-induced
            (high confidence)
land and ocean   frequent
heatwaves
global warming   intensity
heavy precipitation events
    risk of drought   Mediterranean
changes [in] extremes since 1950   extreme
temperatures   heavy precipitation
                              frequency of
droughts
                              resilience of human
long-lasting   irreversible   loss of   ecosystems
                    rapid rise
end of the 21st century
            immediate and unprecedented   global
differences   extremes [are] expected
            higher at 2°C
                    2–3 times greater   regions
with snow or ice
    hot extremes   exceptionally hot days
                    heavy precipitation events [on]
global scale   extreme drought
precipitation deficits
                    water stress   ability of
human systems [to] adapt
food production systems   hazards, exposures, and
vulnerabilities

Small island states

flood hazard   sea-ice-free Arctic Ocean

Global mean sea level rise   slower rate

sea level rise   opportunities for

adaptation   instabilities

triggered   absorbed   anthropogenic

carbon dioxide   acidification

unprecedented   last 65 million   substantial

evidence

adaptation required now

Future risks   mitigation

pathway   occurrence of a transient

overshoot

irreversible loss of some ecosystems

A2 : [searching for answers]

climate change is real shirt

climate change is not caused by humans

climate change is it too late

climate change is evidenced by which of the following

climate change is natural

climate change is caused by

climate change is a natural phenomenon

climate change is good

climate change is the greatest threat

climate change is here

About The Author

JP Seabright is an Activist Archivist residing in the U-Shíyī District of Lúndūn, an area previously known as East London in the former United Kingdom (pre-Sino division and outside the security perimeter). They have dedicated their life to uncovering cultural records of the prelapsarian era, specializing in unpublished proletarian poetry. This is their first anthology.

Acknowledgements

Appearing in their original non-erased versions during the year 2021 C.E./B.F. (Before the Fall) are the following pieces:

Spilt Milk was one of the poems published by the Royal Society of Literature for their Write Across London poetry map of poems written during the first pandemic lockdown.

Reveal-Redact in a fuller form was published by Full House Literary Magazine. Its source material is Chapters 8 and 9 of the Book of Revelation, King James Version of the Bible.

Miasma was published by Punk Noir Magazine.

Weather and [**After Words**] were published in Coven Poetry Journal.

[**ipcc.ch/sr15**] is an erased extract of section 3 of the Intergovernmental Panel on Climate Change (IPCC) Report Global Warming of 1.5°C: Impact of 1.5 °C Global Warming On Natural And Human Systems, published on 9th August in the year 2021 C.E./B.F. (www.ipcc.ch/sr15/)

[**searching for answers**] is the result of a Google Search carried out one month after the publication of the IPCC report.

Praise for the author

"In spare, vivid, and visceral language, JP Seabright imagines the potential consequences of continuing to ignore the current and ongoing climate crisis. By framing *Fragments from Before the Fall* as an anthology of found texts and fragments pieced together contemporaneously by survivors, Seabright allows readers to see from a distance and up close, in medias res. We look on with dread as those battling to endure burn themselves to death, hunt for rats and wait to be devoured. Seabright has juxtaposed apocalyptic horror with tenderness and intimacies: 'black mould' / 'contagious laughter.' The upheaval and disturbance of living through the Fall is reflected in the form of fragments and erasure, the description of pages ripped in half, words drowned by floods or eaten away by fire, the use of Revelation from the Bible to evoke doom and prophesy, the discovery of archives in a waterlogged basement. This doesn't feel speculative because many of the details come from life as we know it: plague, floods, wildfires, loss of ecosystems, later day Capitalism's commodification, ignoring science – we are here, moments away from torture by the end in progress. The Fall is imminent. *Fragments from Before the Fall* is all too likely an accurate prediction. That thought sends a chill through my bones."

Amanda Earl; fallen angel of AngelHousePress and kindred misfit.

"This post-Anthropocene artefact is a post post art fact in which the poet editor of this collection is the archivist of a crisis who has travelled back to meet us from deep within the irretrievable realm of a climate-change-post-place. The Fall is collected and re-presented here in its surviving fragments. The oldest archaeological terms become ones that have not yet arrived, framing the work as a prophecy that documents the 'last/death/chance' for beauty, memory, forgiveness, and perhaps even an apology to the young as their bodies are devoured in the aftermath. Every fight is a breath for survival; the great cow insanity and mass plague open wounds in the first world, a world which is 'hollow/with inarticulation'. There is a vast silence at the heart of this book. The clichés become auto-destructive implosions, refiguring anthems against regret into disaster certainty. The double-tongued toxic effluency of this anthology proclaims 'THE END IS NIGHT'. We have owned the world to death, 'climate change is here', the artefact howls; this is the '[After Party]'."

Cat Chong; Poet, Publisher, Author of *Plain Air: An Apology in Transit*

Praise for the author

"JP Seabright's *Fragments from before the Fall* writes in, through, and after a world 'once green pleasant'. Presented as an anthology, Seabright takes on the role of a curator, taking the reader on a tour of an archive of our contemporary ecological moment through the lens of a speculative future. The fragmented work highlights the holes we have created in the atmosphere, the gaps in our knowledge of environmental science, the ways world governments fall short of the mark in preventing an inevitable climate crisis, and the spaces that will be left after the fall. The experience of reading this collection is like watching a disaster film on rewind while the events rage on just outside the window. Seabright's work offers a pause button, shaking the reader awake to the reality of climate change and our ability to potentially mitigate some of the damage so we don't all become fragments in a post Anthropocene museum."

E.P. Jenkins; Editor, *Coven Poetry*, **Author,** *Rituals* **and** *Rewilding: An Ecopoetic Anthology*